The News Factory

Notes from a Dying City

poems and stories

Matthew Abuelo

Plain View Press

www. plainviewpress.net

1101 W 34th Street, STE 404, Austin, TX 78705

ISBN: 978-1-935514-93-0
Library of Congress Control Number: 2011945370

Cover art and cover design by NOTORIOUS V.I.V.
Book design by Pam Knight

Other collections by Matthew Abuelo
Organic Hotels, ISBN: 978-0-615-16898-2 (2008 Lulu.com)
Last American Roar, ISBN: 978-1-4116-6382-4 (2006 Lulu.com)

Dedicated to those at the Dexter House,

without whose angelic energies,

this book would never have been possible.

Contents

Foreword

It seems to me that a lot of contemporary writing, poetry in particular, relies too heavily on lyricism and self expression at the expense of all substance. People seldom write about their real lives and immediate surroundings any more unless mining outrageous antics for Reality TV shows. In a constant quest for escapism we recoil from what is plainly in front of us, and what was once obvious is now invisible.

In his thoughtful, evocative poetry and short stories, Matthew Abuelo, like Dante Alighieri, takes us on a trip through the underworld of New York City at the beginning of the 21st century and tells the stories of real people clinging like flotsam to the framework of a society weakened by decades of cynicism and neglect.

Matthew dedicated this book to our friends and former neighbors at Dexter House, one of the last residential Single Room Occupancy buildings left on Manhattan's upper west side. In 2004 when the final push came for gentrification and this idiosyncratic refuge was imperiled, we and our fellow "Dexterians" banded together to save the building and fight to preserve it as affordable housing. Two years after we left, the future of our old home and the people who remain there is still uncertain.

The News Factory is a love letter to the people we knew and a testament to all the dreamers, orphans, con-men and hooligans who are still out there somewhere, scratching out a living in a world that stopped listening to them, or even paying attention, a long time ago.

Vivian E. Riffelmacher
New York City
August 1, 2011

Coney Island's Last Stand

No tickets were ever taken here
at the end of the Q line
where prostitutes split in two from the pressure
of choosing a new way to lose.
All rides keep you going in circles
or heading upwards until you hit your peak
then head straight down
past the turnstile into the concrete heart of the animal of consumption
where bloodied fingers beat against
bleached walls
void of graffiti
or a past which is not of New York
but is New York
whose architects know nothing of the garbage heaps
or the pauper's graves
here both are the same for the human wreckage.

The sideshow fancies are swallowed into the
the brown snow soul of the East Coast
and melts into the carnival's last gleaming.

2

The new Indians stand against the oncoming tide that comes to wash
them out of
shared bathrooms like the aborted flow of ghosts of the SRO's
or the Saints of the Dexter House
that learned the art of night diving
onto the reservations of Queens
or washed into the waters of the Hudson down
onto the shores of Coney Island
among the tapestry of newspapers
used condoms
syringes
right into the eye of the storm of human waste
to be buried into the last lights of the people's park.

The Whale Hunt

The voice of the sea is growing silent.
It is quickly becoming canceled in still culture.
The frozen fingers of the sea are tightening around the vocal-cords of its
singers.
The land of the rising sun casts a mute shadow over the arctic symphony.
Harpoons become flaming arrows that pierce the heart of the ancient
song of Ishmael.
There are no more sharks in the water,
they are all on board
with smiles for the canceled meat,
on Wall Street,
in Tokyo
with dollar bills shoved up their noses
waiting for the next snow storm.
Their skin is the images of TV reality
and whose eyes are churches of the voided God of consumption
whose teeth pierce the skin of those Northern Seas
and into the Baghdad sands.
It's shit buries
Coney Island's last stand
or the prostitutes of Time Square's past
whose stomach ingests the genius of descent.

2

What iron hand of industry washes over the northern waters
where the Gemini dagger washes in with the Eastern flow
to know the flesh of the fathers of the sea?

Fly Paper

What are they doing in the Dexter House with their flypaper fancies
stuck in the buzzing mind of three days without sleep
waiting to go to the courts to face the judge
to be betrayed
again.
Who are you
who will look into their eyes and call them ghosts of
the tenements
that the city sleeps to wipe clean
when extinction comes on the wings of the seasons
which bury use under?
Will those who come after recognize your remains from theirs
with currency rotting in the human groin
buried under the concrete which is void of any past?
Or stuck in rooms smaller than the inside of Joe Frazier's swollen nose?
Their passing is the extinction of the city
where even the hangers-on could no longer afford a room at the Chelsea
where Japanese tourists come to see a city bleached of history.
Who among you have learned the art of losing well
to overcome the tension that splits the mind in two
and the newborn skin of heaven and hell falls from view on 86 street.
But never underestimate the lightning of their minds that give rise to
their
young revelatory hearts that overcome
the buzzing fear that they are the new Indians
in their broken down bathrooms
where even the shock to the senses will not wipe them clean
from their rooms.
Twisted Abbots sit alone with gangrene in the leg.
But they will not be digested into the rotten gut of the city
to be shit out on the streets
like another band of American refugees
or vanish into the final frame that festers in the sewers where the other
half
have left their foot prints.
If management survives then something much greater has died.

Pop

Pop spilled over onto the pavement
like the blood of an artist on the fourth floor
and the images that flowered into genius faded like
Coney Island under nightfall.
We are all born as savages,
looking to feed on the weakest of the species
but the doomed will shine in the end
even those who put on high heels and grow old and worry about hiding
their hard-ons in cheap dresses
or dance out the window.
Pop bleaches
turning the New York streets as sexless
as a Catholic's dry dream.
The images as a pop spread as fast as the great pinball machine
and like a quick and painful rash.
Comics became the new art form before the factory doors opened.
Angry dykes in heavy coats in the middle of summer become dangerous
on the fourth floor.
And pop grows well in the Chelsea Hotel but only for those that pass
through
and forget about recreating the American flag.
For all others who chose to stay,
empty eyes become connections to still craniums where nothing lives or
even exists below
and felonies and speed grow stale on the vines of images.
Pop is a dead river.

Radio America

Hello America
Who among you are willing to buy the line of human garbage heaps
that rot under the shadows of old glory
waving upside
down?
And who will buy the line that beats
like a whip
against the thighs of Baghdad
with her aborted flow of
western ideas
civilization,
poetry,
mathematics
and now tears?
Who will deconstruct the lawless night
that comes over the radio waves
where announcers all speak with one voice
that shatters into vacant stations
with dead laughter pumped in
and into the ears of
Riker's,
and the vacant eyes of South Oaks
where blank is beautiful
to avoid the tension of being an animal.

Ok you who control
television sex
that teaches the young to no longer know how be young
and pants suit women to no longer know how to be women.
Who among you are worthy to walk in the dreams of old men?
You who have become separated from your nature like
a stillborn wrapped in newspaper and dumped in the back alleys
of dead hospitals.
Do you know your nature?
Can you understand it?

Do you really believe that you can control the ocean?
How much was the price for Christ when you sold it
to those who only know surrender?
What is more dangerous than a man with nothing to lose?
Who smiles with the accomplishment
of striking the first stake that gave rise to Coney Island
or the underground railroad
or Wall Street
or the American ghetto?

Who sold
Jerusalem?
What price is Christ in Chinatown
and did you get crabs from fucking
the Baghdad sands
to erase time with rancid ejaculation?
The blank mind
is beautiful
when senses are fragmented.
Who among you will sever
your rotting connections to the
black fruit that expands
under the last days of ancient sunlight
and under the sands of holy
Babylon?
The last words of your film
as Burroughs said
"Play it all
Play it all
Play it all back
Pay it all
Pay
It
all
back."

2

What hour are you in
11:59?
The time is later than you think
In the eye of the final burning Buddha
Or old glory's last gleaming
The Subway Serenade,
"Ladies and gentlemen I'm homeless and I have AIDS…"
Did you know that your icons
have honed the art of homicide to a fine point
that comes with a single flash
to wipe clean that which you could not
force to dance in peep shows
in Hell's Kitchen?
Blank is beautiful
when the price splits
the Mind in two.

3

Do you know Lou Hill,
the abbot of the airwaves,
whose visions capture
Ginsberg,
Hoffman,
Vonnegut,
Bob Fass
and whose ears and heart
were the ears and hearts of a revolution?
What fold in time took the great saint of the radio
to fade into footsteps of those who die young?
"This Genius Has Been Withdrawn"
as Watson said.
There is only so far that the last waters could drag you under.
The strip show
of the naked American politics
which lack all features
of being human
with all its parties
being one party
that fills its groin with death and
grows wild on the great human wreckage.

4

GE
What sorrowful song have you sung for the Hudson
Which you have violated with your chemical finger
Our great sister who watches over us on the upper Westside.

Untitled

Everything that I know
I have stolen from those places
where the angels of neurosis hide
fragmented childhoods
that they have yet to breakdown.
Nor have they formed a new metabolic system
to digest the fit and the fury that seeps out of
genius
born
of a life that fits in a garbage bag
to
be placed in front of
SROs
shared bathrooms
and roach hotels
and woken by the beating of steam pipes
in the dead of winter.
The expiration date
of what we owe expires
when our feet hit the concrete.
The mediator
between the Dexter House
and skid row
are the fractured personalities
of the last mole people.
What remains is
the
brown snow
of what is left behind
only to fade into the theater's
last gleaming
To be found 10 days later
as the smell reaches the hallways
and their diamonds shatter into the
light.

Risking Absurdity

There are just so many times that you can risk absurdity
making deals with dead art forms
recalled
when you hit rock bottom
in an effort
to rise where the angels place their bets on
how the energy of the city will break
and wash over the fragmented faces of the grid
before we are slammed down onto the concrete
under the shadow of millionaires row
of 86th street
down into the subway stations
and through the turnstiles
where the homeless
pick through the lost tickets
to recuperate some of what they gambled
away.
This is where they scream the name of Jesus
and profanities before they give their voice over
to the metallic screech
of the cars that pass.
But they fade into the soundboard
where the other beggars sing off-key
and they know that there will be no weeping wall or
Jerusalem for those who die under the watchful eye of
Rabbi roach and Father rat who tend to their bones,
before they are sent to Potter's Field
where even the sick flower of industry fails to digest
with its perfect mockery
all that remains of the
parade of the doomed.

Red Light District of the Heart

Do know that we wait in window fronts
for those on the others side of the glass
in the red light district of the
heart?

We unfasten our belts
like a centrifuge,
tiny explosions cross all borders
inside
where anxieties are born in afterhour hotels
where lunatics scream in bathrooms down the hallways
of lonely fags.
What is it that you don't understand?

This is no dance of the silhouette of
Philippe Petit on the high wire
to be seen when the fog finally breaks.
Down here
the wind is far too vulgar
with its touch that sends the city reeling.
Did you know that we undress in the bathrooms
down the hall
where we devolve into roach hotel pasts
and dreams of life under the floorboards
or return to the sea where we were born?

Lou Hill

Why did you turn out the light
before we found our way to the
top of the garbage heap?
Nor do we hear the seagulls that now feed
on a humor born of a current of genius
which shoots up a brittle cord?
Have we broken the habit of
casting the water boys
over the edge to
the wards
where the waters of the Euphrates finally breaks?
Your dream flowered in Houston
before being incinerated
in the kkk sun,
only to be rebuilt.
Your carnival
of voices broke through the
static of dead radio waves
Where is Bob Fass???

Revolution of Trash

Did you know that we dream of winter
to bury the fear of what is behind the door
what we let come through that door,
or
to know that we all die at an equal speed
or feed
grey subway station lunatics
who dream on the 6th floor
in the mockery of their own larval skin.
The key lies in the disappearing act from bus station
to silent hallways
to bathrooms five steps from rooms in SROs
to NyQuil dreams that move in reverse
and revolutions of swirling trash.
This you will not understand.
The ruin you will know is always etched in skin
like a signature burned into our sins.
There is no more sleeping under the floorboards of 86th street.
We've reached the surface far too late
to be met by the Hudson winds
or the cries of the new Indians
whose backs are always to the river.
To lift the thumb of each landlord
that snaps the spines of Brazilian Dykes who trade scrap iron for
cash
or invalids whose minds reverberate
like a gloved hand in the wake of a felony,
screaming mad,
or drift off into Saint Luke's
where all peace shatters like glass.
What eyes are connected to minds that
flower in the electric storms of shock treatment,
to know flesh as the new meat for bed bugs
or to be sold on the auction block.
What skin will you wear?

2

Will you know the Jerusalem of their hearts?
those of the Dexter house
who travel in time
of fading New York
not as travelers
but as pictures
of that what once was
or of saints of the SROs,
in their perfect skin
as they breathe the sweet air of frantic voices
"Rico do you want some coffee?!"
How many more times must they crawl for you?
How many more times can they offer roach-eyed clarity,
and you offer them only your mockery
you of the corners of West 86th street.
How many times must they live under the floor boards for you
the corrections officer whose brother lives in Queens
and whose final treasure is death from his own hand,
fear fading in the ever expanding light,
or the Canadian Buddhist who knows prayer
not on her knees but in dance
and whose mantra is called beauty.
And how many more of their words will you step over
only to get swept up into the crude tide
of landlords who wait in doorways for those ghosts
who remind them that the city will always swallow its own tail.
No one is above the food chain.
Here the bedbugs and roaches are royalty.

3

You will not understand the old union leader
who chants the phrases of Walt Whitman
whose heart is that of Whitman and whose soul is of Solomon.
What words will you understand of the frantic musician who
is not of the city
but is the city.
These pictures will never fade
like so many newspapers at your feet.
Will you understand?
Will you know the revolution of trash?

Goodbye Sergeant

It was the first day of spring and the season for the tombs to send convicted prisoners upstate to serve their prison sentences had just begun. The bus had just arrived to pick up the men who were now being warehoused for pickup. Sergeant William Horowitz walked down the room of the holding cells, followed by two larger policemen, one with a shotgun held tightly against his breast. Inside the first cell was a tall black kid, who was no older than eighteen, wearing his blue jeans just high enough to cover his crotch, and a white sleeveless tee-shirt. The kid had a long jagged scare on one cheek from what William could only assume was from a fight or being jumped by fellow kids from his neighborhood.

"Ok son, grab the bars, your ride is here." William remarked with a bored tone in his voice.

This job had become so routine, he knew what response to expect from each prisoner based on the look in their eyes. The kid straightened up to display his full height in an empty attempt to intimidate his jailers. The kids face was hardened but his eyes showed the same fear as those animals who know their end was around the corner or down some long corridor.

"You white mother fuckers sold my black ass to them upstate hicks! No black man gets a break in this country for nuthin. Congratulations cop, you got your prized nigga. Things never fuckin' change".

"Yes it's all the white man's fault you're here. Had nothing to do with that cannon you blasted into the clerk's chest at the bodega I suppose."

"I didn't shoot no fuckin clerk, your boys grabbed the first nigga they could find to set up for this bullshit. What you need a suspect, your boys come to the Bronx and grab the first brother they could find? That damn judge and everyone in the court room knows I didn't have nuthin to do with that clerk getting shot."

"Well you're the winner of the lottery then, grab the bars."

"Man, I got set up I'm telling you! I'm innocent, man. Listen to me!"

"Is that why they found your finger prints on the gun left at the scene? Look Reggie, we're just holding you here. The judge set the sentence and he is god in that court room. Now hurry up I don't have all day."

Before the kid could protest further, the cop with the shot gun cocked the barrel. The argument had suddenly ended. The kid grabbed the bars as William opened the jail doors and the guards entered shackling the prisoner's wrists and ankles. He was frog walked a few feet out of the cage then was taken by another guard to a hallway just outside the room.

William walked two cells down where he was greeted by an older and heavily tattooed biker with long white hair which rested on a leather vest which was a size too small for the biker's frame. His back was pressed against the far wall of the cell with one booted foot supporting him the other leg was bent and his foot rested on the wall. He was thin and strangely pale with a yellow tint. The skin of his face was stretched tight over his sharp cheek bones giving the biker the look of an old Indian.

"Back again Sal? What are you in for now?"

"Had a talk with some little shit bartender. You know the kind. Some little twenty something shithead ain't goin to talk to nobody no more."

"You mean you beat the kid to death while on crystal meth? What was the argument about there?"

"I told him to turn up the volume on the tv behind the bar, baseball game was on and I told that mother I had fifty bucks on the game. That little piece of shit acted as if he didn't hear me. I know he heard me when I pulled his ass across the bar before I beat the shit out of him with my bar stool."

"Well Sal you're going to have plenty of time to watch the game where you're going. You know the routine. Let's get on with it."

The biker walked to the front of the cell and grabbed the bars and once again William opened the jail door and the two guards shackled the prisoner's wrists and ankles. Two other guards came in and marched him down the hall.

William moved on to the next cell. In the cage was a tranny-professional woman. He/she wore a miniskirt with high heel shoes. Her long blond hair fell loosely on her shoulders while strands were caught up in the caked makeup which, along with a five o'clock shadow and deep lines in her face gave her the look of old New York with its hopeless avenues which provided such women with a career.

"Says here you're here for offing a John."

"No I would never do that, I'm a professional girl. I treat all my customers well. I'm a woman who gives these men something extra if you know what I mean. You believe me, don't you?"

"Why did they find you with the guy's wallet?"

"Oh I found it on the ground. I wanted to make sure he got it back. I was going to mail it back to him."

"What an empty wallet"?

"What people do with their stuff is none of my business."

"Why did they find the John's body with a switch blade in his jugular, seven blocks from where you were picked up"?

"Was he? Oh that's terrible, I would never do such a thing. Never!"

"Well the jury sent your sweet ass upstate. Besides I have no say about it."

"Says here you were in Bellevue. What were you in the nut house for?"

"My rooommate called 911 telling them I was tryin' to kill myself. Can you imagine? She said I was slashing my wrists. That's so crazy."

"Is that the reason for the marks on your arms?"

"No that was from some fuckin' john who got too rough."

"I think you've cracked a long time ago but that's for the doctor's up state to decide."

He sighed deeply then moved onto the next cell. In the fourth and final cell set to be emptied, sat a painfully thin Honduran whose face was in his hands, weeping deeply.

"Christ, Juan, you're in here again? What you like this place so much? What are you in for this time?"

The man looked up with tears still streaming from his eyes. He attempted to smile a toothless smile but the gesture only made him look more broken down.

"I beat my wife I was drunk and so mad."

"Well you'll have all the time you need to dry out. Why did you hit your old lady, Juan?"

"I found her sleeping with my best friend. She's a cheating bitch you know."

"You two will have a break from each other then."

"What is your immigration status?"

"I'm legal got my green card."

"You mean you got an expired card?"

"No sergeant. Everything good with the card."

"I hope so for your case."

William walked out of the room and passed the waiting prisoners and then outside for a cigarette. Normally the questioning would happen the night before the convicts were sent upstate. But the boredom of the job and a vague trepidation of seeing the men's faces led him to conduct the business later than anyone was accustomed. It was already late March but the fallen and blackened snow was frozen solid in four foot mounds along the sidewalk. He didn't hate any of the men he sent upstate, nor did he feel guilty about seeing the group leave, that part of him died a long time ago. William was every bit the prisoner as the ones being led out into the freezing air. He heard the whispers around him from all the other officers.

No officer in the station trusted him as no sergeant is trusted in any precinct in New York City or Long Island. He was always going to be the outsider giving orders he knew would surely be ignored. When any of his guys shot a kid down, he felt the noose around his neck tighten as the television stations demanded answers from him. All the while there were forever officers sitting in diners crucifying him as being just another clueless asshole who accepted the hated job of "Sergeant".

"Yeah the sergeant is a douchebag. Screw that guy, I'm here for a few more months then I'm taking the detective' test. I ain't going to have to listen to that asshole anymore. He thinks he knows what's going on..."

He was too old to take the test himself and he was the only one stupid enough to accept the sergeant's job. So there was nowhere for him to go but retire and that was still five years away. He reached into his pants pocket and pulled out a single cigarette followed by a zippo lighter. He breathed in the first drag, long and slow then exhaled a plume of smoke which dissipated into the gray frozen sky.

William looked around outside the station at the ever changing city. Just outside of view was the diner where he got his first cup of coffee as a rookie. It was later replaced by a Pottery Barn and now was nothing more than an empty store front. Gone too were the white knuckled cops who strong armed the hookers and shook down gang bangers for drugs and money. Now he was surrounded by amateurs, often busting black kids for smoking joints in the parks or clamping down on the homeless and the hopeless who sleep in Pen Station. Many of these kids were brutal meter maids, bringing in anyone when there was a need for overtime or the ennui of boredom became too great. Gone were the honest payoffs that allowed the professional girls to continue to walk the streets and the police to eat well. All the girls now worked for agencies which advertised in the back of the Village Voice or Chinese massage parlors. Today's police force, William sadly surmised, was on the dollar of landlords of SROs who brought in thugs for hire to clear out their buildings. Many of them (the thugs for hire) had grown used to being residents of boiler rooms where immigration was none the wiser of their presence. He had long grown tired of reading in the papers of the bored brutality committed by cops in the Bronx, Staten Island or Brooklyn. There was hardly a week when a suspect was not shot down in the tenements or found among piles of trash bags. But in the heart of Manhattan, the real estate was as clean as ancient Rome. The outer boroughs became the hinterlands to the great shining city, occupied by the pretty and the immaculate faced children living off of massive trust funds.

William closed his eyes, feeling a migraine coming on. He was greeted by the lightless room that had become all too familiar. There were to be no dreams in this windowless room. Not those which come at night or otherwise. There were no shadows anywhere which came as a mercy. For he feared all shadows for the same reason all cops fear shadows. It is the fear of meeting all those they had a hand in sending upstate; there was the small time pot dealer, the prostitute caught up in a Chinese raid and all the youths who enter the system without fangs. What returned were beaten and raped wolves of the penitentiary system. Prison has always been the criminals training camp.

Somewhere a radio was playing. He couldn't tell if it was in the back of his cranium of from some unseen car,

> *I've got ::cling cling:: fsssss steam heat.*
>
> *I've got ::cling cling:: fsssss steam heat.*
>
> *But I need your love to keep away the cold.*
>
> *I've got ::cling cling:: fsssss steam heat.*
>
> *I've got ::cling cling:: fsssss steam heat.*
>
> *I've got ::cling cling:: fsssss steam heat.*
>
> *But I can't get warm without your hand to hold.*

"What kind of old savage bastard could be playing that forgotten goddam song now"? For the pressure building in his head was not unlike the steam that comes through the pipes before leaving the radiators in a hiss. That song was coming from the back of the furthest recess of his mind. William laughed softly, a defeated laugh. The deafening sound of heavy bass and rhythmic ramblings from a passing car drowned out the sound of Williams radio. He opened his eyes to see the last of the prisoners being ushered in on a bus.

He looked up and there high above the city a golden light shone down on him. He knew it was not holy, but neither was he.

"Look!" He cried. "My ship has finally come in."

Untitled

Do you know the language of the Dexter House?
It is built on tears and the mantra called beauty.
Those who speak it belong to a tribe which lives between
the bathrooms down the hall
and the perimeter
of what once was.
Will you not bend to their touch,
which was born of genius
or walk through their doors
to taste the bitter fruit
of losing
well?
And then to be forgotten?
You must earn the right to speak this new language
that rings through the hallways like bells at midnight.
Each word is formed in the neon wilderness
where the show of shows lies in ruins
like those theaters
who show her
my sister
the animal of instinct
in heat.
The breath of the Dexter House will break through the floorboards
in this living museum of brilliance
in a new battle hymn.
The tongue to speak this language
has a recoil which throws each outcast
against the walls
of their rooms
where you are always too close to falling out the window.
Each ounce of meaning doubles as
the weight of fortune
turns back on you
like the flames that beat against your thighs
while dancing in fire.

Night Diving

The gravity of each note when
you strike the right chord
will always pull you under
where the river of fortune turns back on you
with remorseless passion
to appear as a strange mark
under the lens of an X ray
or leaves you naked under the
bright lights of the show of shows.
then leaving you
crawling on a bandaged knee in the closets of ex-lovers
or to the end of the road of dead things
where emotion sleeps
in silence
at the tables
of penny bars
of that which is forgotten.
Did you know the brilliance of
each show that dissolves on your tongue
only to recede below the waterline.
The distance of what once was will
always expand
and in between we sit as nameless assholes
at a feast of fools
dreaming of the ghosts who dance along the skyline
just out of reach.
Nothing that explodes lasts for very long.

2

The door you will know
will lead you to that show of shows which
sends you twirling
with steps that grow
more narrow
like a silhouette on a high wire over the city
with the first break of the fog.
The love that returns from this distance
is a silk screen
image which is its skin
with nothing living below.
If she was to return to you
Pray she remembers this dance.

Untitled

It's the greatest fight you'll ever know
to breath through unclenched teeth
or live in a skin not made of winter
when that brown snow finally melts
all that remains
is a voice kept on ice
only to melt into
the sounds of each subway station which comes through
and flickers.
This is when your life flushes out into the backwash of
the last of the sewage born from those memories of her
which dances over the roof tops
among the antennas
like a marionette who finally learned to cut himself loose.
It's silhouette vanishing behind your eyelids
as you see the city through candle light
swaying to the notes of 1930's back alley blues bars.
That face at the bottom of the bottle
is your reflection
as everything you know falls from view
and each detail distorts
and recedes into a negative
which can only be seen through the last light of clarity.

2

This is night diving in ever expanding heights
to reach so far below for those things we have saved
like obsessed abbots in the hysteria of an opium dream.
Darkness will always hide what we've forgotten
and when you realize the safety is gone
it's too late.
This gravity leaves fear naked and wet
only to dissolve into bitterness as harsh
as saltwater in the lungs.
Sooner or later you will realize that emotion is
for rent
and every landlord constantly comes to collect.

3

When she walked through your door
when you let her through that door
the warning was sitting there waiting for you
like death smiling behind your eyelids
or a sign that lets you know that
that the net has been removed from so far below.
And her
and your love
has a recoil which shatters all silence
like glass.
But your husband had just died
before you were swallowed
into her room which was never meant for two.
And that last jump you realize
you will be met by a gravity that will never change.
It is the one constant
as the word the animal of instinct
distorts
forcing all other emotions to sleep
like strange creatures in the dead of winter.
And this bitterness is best taken with the cheapest of wines.
And you realize that every fall
always leads back to you.

Untitled

This is no Halloween parade in the wild night
where you can hide from yourself
in costumes made of those emotions
which wash back on you like a sewage drain off Coney Island.
This is no theater
where every door leads to silent stages
where mute performers cast off the loveless winter
in the seasons of their emotions.
The gravity that pulls you under that
stage
where you dance with those who want you the most
only to be denied
with a flicker of your sneer.
The affliction of your love
is only for those who invite you to
rooms never meant for two
but only for a little a while.
This gravity is the only consistency that you will ever know.
If you knew that your fall has only begun,
after dancing on the head of a pin
would you still have swallowed those pills
or lost yourself in the timeless moments of Asia?
You should have known that the only bottom of that bottle
is the sick mornings that come in reverberations
and static
as loud as unseen bees that nest behind your eyes
those fuckin' bees
and the noise
which is burned into the mockery of the day
and the trains that pass always head west.

2

You could have gotten out
but decided to recede into
that town which breaks down your perfect skin
which is always ripe under the shadow of that
whip that lies limp between your brother's jaw
like an unforgiving tongue which never
misses its mark,
or to live under the shadow of the abandoned watch factory
which sits like death in the middle of another breakdown.
Night diving is a game of chance
when you finally figure out what is below it's always too late to turn back
and what remains is the banal static of television sets
the regret of stripping for those who you hate now.
There was the junkie who shoved the rock up your nose.
Then there was the Dyke
from Oklahoma who survived the Navy
only to go adrift in all the local bars
and ignore the winds that try to push her back to land.
None of the straight girls can deny her
especially the married ones.
She came calling that long and faithful night
when the breakdown took you by the throat like a lover,
bound and gagged.
Every light through your window
you swore he was coming home.
But there was no way to preserve what was lost
in that fall
to save
like any antique to be sold alongside the Coney Island Fortune teller at
Billy's.
There is no admission fee to enter
your show of shows
(which sits just beyond the bright lights of the city)
only a willingness to lose
well.

Visions of the Future

When will we see the renaissance of vision
not in a political skin
but
with true understanding?
Down here on the second floor
we watch the future on a television screen
with faulty reception.
On 96th street
protestors gather in front of Saint Luke's to
demand the release of Abraham
who has been on 24 hour suicide watch
after trying to kill his son.
When I first moved to the city,
I sat in the bathroom down the hall
with a case of the shingles
before I passed a stone.
Each room of the Dexter House
throws each pauper to the present
where they wait with the open nerve anticipation
or lay on silent beds
next stop Potter's field.
This is the animal
of the future
which swims upstream in the Hudson
its belly filled with the nameless assholes
of the sidewalks.
There was the former model from
Glamour magazine
1983
who was found on 91st street.
She wanders in the time of AIDS.
She was 50 but looked twice that.
Frank lived on 87th street
among piles of newspapers and
photo albums
I'd rather die than give up my memories,
he lamented.

Last time anyone saw him was by Lincoln Center
with all his things in garbage bags.
Eddie was found after an overdose
while Lucy gave in to cancer.
They found her 10 days later
according to all the rumors.
Russell squatted all over town
kept a flaming monk under his tongue
to find something to stand for.
Twenty years later
he blew his mind out on drugs.
Now he is looking for a movement
in ghosts
while living out of his car.
And the Frenchman who lives in clothes and a skin
that is never quite clean now lies in his room
on the 6th floor
among his books and writings
growing drunk on box wine
and thoughts of a woman that's no longer there.
And his dreams
which never come in clear are always a reminder that
he
never
made
The Scene.
Now he tries to make love
with his midnight breakdowns
born of rejections from those
who live on the other side of the door.

Helena almost faded into the shelters
after a judge sold her up the river
let the landlord throw her out
into the coldest day of the year.
Small victory
politician put her back
in her room.

2

Are there no lighthouses for those ghosts of the tenements
sidewalks
and scaffolding
that swim against the Hudson tide
only mournful groans from passing barges?

3

At heart we have grown as snake dancers
attempting to tame
the seasons of our ruin
which we wear like a tattoo
burned into our skin
by fire.
Do you want to survive this hidden cinema
which despite the words spoken in each frame
comes on like a silent movie
with its dramatic score
whose villains still surf the sewage of the Hudson?

4

Not every star will be
assassinated by the photographer's lens
to be trapped in still time that is
no time
which knows no time.
The former model dead on 91st street
Roberto whose mind is being wiped clean
as new stone
on medicine cocktails
and dying in unequal parts.
There's the stripper who
still dry-humps the scene
and anyone
under the neon forest
who is willing to pay.
This is the
final call,
the last show.
The price of admission is
just becoming too high.

Untitled

Who are these faces that walk in the gray light of the city
along the equatorial lines of the grid?
Who are these names
which seep from the section doors of SROs
only to be pressed in still
time
where old ghosts still sit at diner counters
waiting
with cups of coffee on stained napkins.

You will not understand
blood thirsty cops
from long island
unravel their flypaper
to catch the natives of
the tenements
under the wild moon
only to dump them into the psych wards of Saint Luke's.
This is the opera of the SROs
last take of a city that has turned back on itself
the final number before the lights go out on the crowd.
The shelters are open again.
Your landlord
sleeps with the souls of janitors
looking to wipe
the building clean
the genius
of unprofitable ideas
plucking each one
like rubies
off the subway tracks
as the strap hangers
watch you fade into a blur
as the city bus passes
under
the neon night
where

rooms
once
used for locals
are now
full again
with tourists.

On the Passing of Jim Carroll

That which does not heal
cuts in the other direction
and Jim
you crawled through that
slit on Christ's side
only to be bled
into a city of junk
and art
where you slept at the Chelsea hotel
or worked the desk
at the factory.
The sick morning
can finally relax its hand from
your throat
in this
the season of your passing.
Now that your keyboard has grown silent
even the air weeps
not being able to taste your words
which were
precise
somehow delicate
but no less savage.
I know
that you dance among those
stars in a New York sky
hidden by the light so far below
from 42nd street
Astor place
Alphabet city.
or Chelsea.
But now your
words come down like rain
in the pages
of a novel not yet released
or performances
forgotten
or your last show at the Bottom Line.

But each mind that knew you
or your art
will turn back on themselves
that you have passed from
view
like the last fruit fly
in the early morning sunlight.

The Bus Terminal

Harvey Gray stood on the corner of 45th Street and 9th Avenue on his way home from his archivist job where he stored media coverage from around the country, usually news of the blackest nature. After a while, each story merged into one long string of static,

"12 year old girl was kidnapped out of her family's home. Earlier today another Senator was found to have received funding from questionable sources. 23 year old Bronx woman was found raped and murdered earlier today. And now sports" and so on.

By the end of the day he would find himself close to another breakdown. The isolation in which he worked only added to the weight of his slow daily unraveling which usually ended hours after he got home. At night, he would see the images and hear the voices becoming one long stream until it was as if he was watching a film from an unseen projector. Harvey would wake up in a cold sweat as it dawned on him that he had no idea where to go with his life. Truth was that he never pictured himself working in an office; it was a position in which he found himself out of necessity. He could never quite hack skid row. He was too responsible. He could live in a roach infested apartment but needed to know how he was going to pay his rent.

Taxi cabs, SUVs and semis were stopped on the crosswalks forcing pedestrians to walk blindly around the trucks, into oncoming traffic heading west to the highway. Two blocks away one could hear the constant honking of the horns from Wall Street gamblers on their way back to New Jersey. Harvey looked up at the traffic light impatiently it had been green for some time. A few people around him were nearly hit by cars speeding down the narrow roads. Just as the light was turning yellow, Harvey found himself jumping backwards to avoid a bicycle delivery boy who seemed to be unwilling to stop for anyone or anything in front of him.

"Lousy bastard," he muttered to himself.

With a deep sigh, he continued to make his way through the slow mulling crowds of tourists and locals as they stepped out of tiled hallways and onto the sidewalk. On a few occasions, Harvey found himself behind someone who stopped walking then stood in the middle of the sidewalk while crowds moved clumsily round them.

"Not a good place to stop," Harvey sneered.

The only responses came in the form of dead-eyed apathy or dumbfounded surprise that anyone would question such autistic disconnection from the world around them. He passed a group of neighborhood kids with hardened faces and perfect brutality in their eyes. Despite all attempts to make Hell's Kitchen family friendly, most of the area stayed true to its nature, with its strip bars and sex shops with private booths where live girls still performed for anyone willing to pay. Late at night, dealers still attempted to sell drugs and women to the young out-of towners. And the cops continue to ignore any and all transactions.

As he made his way uptown, the crowds started to thin out considerably and the faces of the store fronts changed from high end restaurants and Deli chains to takeout Mexican and Chinese joints and a bike rental business. In front of a Laundromat, it's owner usually sat in a lawn chair. Every summer he would wear little more than exposed varicose veins, a pair of sunglasses, shorts that were a size too small for his frame and an old tee shirt with holes in the chest. Next to him lay a large blue dog that would walk inside anytime the crowd became too heavy. This was not one of those days. Harvey passed by quickly with the hope of beating the light of 57th street. He had no such luck as he stepped off the curb and onto the crosswalk with his heels hugging the metal of a drain.

As he stood there once again waiting for the light to change, a taxi ran a red light in front of a red Chevy Chevette Scooter with white racing stripes. The driver of the Chevette swerved to avoid hitting the cab but sideswiped an old man standing too far from the curb, throwing him to the ground with a broken hip. Then the vehicle slammed straight into Harvey, whose bottom half became stuck onto the grill and was carried across the side walk and straight into a concrete wall.

Harvey was pinned between the car and the wall, while he scanned the world around him. Bystanders watched screaming but there was no sound; it was as if their voices had been canceled. The trucks and cars which passed also seemed to have grown mute. Harvey noticed that his lower half was fused with the Chevette as if he had become one with man's invention. He looked through the windshield of the car. The driver was a heavy set woman, paralyzed with fear. Her mind still coming to terms with the fact that she had swerved to avoid one disaster only to create another. As the world around him faded to black, one voice was able to penetrate the absolute silence, "This guy splattered like a grapefruit when he hit that wall! Holy shit!"

In the middle of the darkness, a single white dot pulsed and expanded. A room of type writers could be heard and then seen as the white dot filled the black void. Suddenly the tapping of the keys stopped and silence replaced the metallic noise. The scene faded and gave way to a blue tunnel where Harvey could hear the sound of the express A train heading downtown.

He awoke with a start, finding himself standing in line in front of a teller's window. He let out a scream of utter confusion. The room was awash in a bluish white light, like that of an old terminal. The hall itself was vast with waiting areas that lined long walkways where dead eyes stared at monitors. In between the gates were what looked like gift shops and bars, filled with waiting bodies. The buzzing of neon lights filled the air.

A voice shot out from overhead, *"All new arrivals should refrain from screaming. Please be courteous to those around you!"*

He tried peering around those in front of him to see how much longer he would have to wait. Everyone stood straight as though acting on instinct. He finally tapped an old man on the back of the shoulder, "Hey man do you know what this line is for?" The stranger replied with a Brooklyn accent, "I dunno. I think it's to find out where the hell we're s'pose ta go, I guess. There's never anyone around ta help you, damn kids today. Sorry Mac."

The old man then looked down mournfully and then turned back around. A sea of voices ebbed and flowed. A loud banging rang out as steam shot through unseen pipes. Moments later, a hissing sound permeated the thick air. Several announcements, in various languages came from unseen speakers throughout the terminal.

"Passengers to Olympia, Washington, your bus will be arriving at gate 2C, again your bus will be arriving at gate 2C."

"Пассажиры идя к Москва ваша шина теперь всходит на борт на стробе 75A"

"Passengers to Limbo, your bus will be arriving at gate 5D."

As Harvey stood in the line, he felt a sudden numbing concern, "What was this place? Was he killed in the accident?" Before he could reach a conclusion about his predicament he found himself being called to a teller's window. A dark skinned woman with a broad face, high cheek bones and a heavy build sat behind thick glass with only a computer and a stack of paper to give an appearance of an official station.

"What's your name?" she asked.

"Harvey Gray."

She looked him up and down for a second then gave him paperwork to fill out. Harvey looked down and noticed that the forms were in Spanish.

He turned around and approached the window once again. A nervous Frenchman who had just got done adjusting his belt and shirt tapped Harvey on the shoulder and began to speak in broken sentences. "Excuse me but I was next!" he said, his index finger pointing straight up. "It's my turn to go! Its illegitimate people like you who just cut in..."

Harvey hardly gave notice as he tried to get the tellers attention. "Excuse but I don't read Spanish." The woman gave a disgusted sigh, looked at the form and then handed him another one.

"Sit down and fill these out. Come back up here when you're done."

He turned around to find a place to sit, Harvey noticed the stranger who had failed to get his attention. He was thin with sunken eyes. His lips formed barely a sliver of an opening. A near colorless tongue covered with a white film kept licking the corners of his mouth in a nervous twitch.

Harvey found a seat in the corner of a rundown bar. The floors were made of splintering wood and covered with saw dust and the lighting gave the room the appearance of a schooner's underbelly. Those who sat at the tables spoke with heavy Irish accents and looked like characters from Ellis Island photos from the early 1900's. The walls were covered with black and white photos from old New York. A blackboard had a list of different cheeses along with light and dark beer. Harvey ordered what the bartender referred to as a round, which was simply two beers, a light and a dark.

 He grabbed his drinks and then walked over to his table. He filled out the forms, which were straightforward; first and last name, language spoken at home, country of origin, cause of death, any chance you survived, preferred place to be sent, and so on. When he reached the question, "cause of death", a deep embarrassment came over him. How could anyone admit to being killed by a fucking Chevy Chevette?

"Shit," he thought, "that's worse then being killed by a Pinto. Surely an exploding gas tank is a better way to go than getting hit by a tin can on wheels."

He looked up and found a message carved into the wall. "The tears that you cried yesterday are now downriver. The tide at your feet knows no such sorrow." The embarrassment began to fade. He realized that he was now playing one of his usual head games to explain away that which made him look foolish. With that he signed the papers and added one last note.

"Why would I try to be God before I mastered the art of being human?" Harvey jotted down with a grin on his face. Without realizing that he didn't touch either of his beers, Harvey ran out of the bar and straight to the window. Another round of announcements came from overhead.

"Los pasajeros que van a San Juan su autobús ahora está saliendo de la puerta 118B."

"Passengers going to Tallahassee, your bus will be arriving at gate 150D."

When he made it back to the window, the teller looked over the forms. When she reached the middle of the page, her eyebrows rose. She leaned over to another teller and both started laughing. Harvey couldn't hear what was being said but was well aware of what was behind the humor which brought both women to a state of hysterics. The teller wiped the tears from her eyes and handed him a ticket which read, "One Way to 345 West 86 street room 204." As it turned out, that was Harvey's residence.

"Does this mean I survived the crash?" he asked.

"Oh my heavens no! You were cut in half by that car honey," the teller said while trying to hide her laughter. "This ticket is for your room at the hotel, where you are to stay for as long as the building is there."

"And after that?" Harvey asked.

"You have to ask another agent, that's not my job," the teller said, now calling up the next person in line.

"You've got to be kidding me!" he screamed. This was his home for the past fours years with his wife Sophia and two cats. The room was 15 by 13 feet and cluttered mostly with his wife's garbage, which spanned over twelve years, her possessions consisting of clothing, newspapers, movie cases, painting supplies and knick knacks found in arcades and museums. At night, the roaches lay claim to the walls with little fear of being exposed to the light. Harvey would spend his nights crushing the larger ones slowed by old age. Dirt had covered the windows, which made it difficult to decipher the time of day without a clock, theirs usually ran half an hour fast. He was glad to spend the time with Sophia. Would she join him after her death or would she go elsewhere? It was a question that Harvey had no idea about and it was apparent that the teller wasn't going to tell him, even if she knew.

"When is the next bus?" he asked.

"I don't know," she replied. "Whenever it gets here."

He shoved the ticket in his pants pocket, then walked down the trail of gates, gift shops and bars. Each waiting room was a world unto itself. Within the first, a group of Christians ripped crosses from around their necks and threw them on the floor, yelling and hissing about how they had wasted their lives trying to follow a being that they now knew was nothing more than a child's fairy tale. The oldest member of the group just sat there with a red face, droplets of spittle around his mouth. An announcement rang out in a language that Harvey didn't understand but figured was telling those waiting for the next trip out of the station that their bus had just arrived. The old man stood up and walked out of the room without looking at the others or Harvey for that matter. Such a scene would have given Harvey a certain sense of satisfaction before his death. Quite often he and the others passing through the 59th street subway station would be verbally assaulted by Caribbean women, demanding that those within ear shot repent.

The 42nd street station was the usual gathering spot for the Baptists who handed out flyers but were not as vocal as others. Along the wall leading to the Broadway train, signs lined the walkway with quotes from the bible, "There will be no God before me" and so on. For the most part, Harvey found that avoiding eye contact was sufficient to repel any overtures from the Baptists. But those at Union Square park would cause him to gnash his teeth.

There were two that stood out above the small group. The heavyset young preacher would engage the audience with the skill of a used car salesmen. To prove his point, he would mix the teaching of Jesus and other sections of the new Testament with pieces of science that he read in one article or another, often getting the lesson wrong and in the end improvising the rest of the speech. It was an ingenious model of the modern snake oil salesman. But it was really the skinny kid who had a look in his eye of one who was on 24 hour suicide watch that made Harvey's skin crawl. Unlike his contemporary who used humor and quasi-science, he appeared to fall into a trance, his mind taken over by the waters of the biblical floods as it fell twelve leagues under the cross. All that was missing were the tattered robes. He would scream each twisted word of warning, oblivious to the onlookers who mocked him as though he were grateful for the abuse. His words were far more savage and designed to systematically break down those unfortunate enough to listen.

"You stand there speaking with idle words!" he would shout. "Do you really hate his message so much that you will mock it? It says in the Bible that the end will come when all nonbelievers mock his word!" Usually he was met with indifference or shouts and hisses from bystanders.

In Times Square, old men and women with their daughters from the Midwest held signs that ranged from the single word, "Pray," or to the more prophetic, "The End is Near."

But despite his distaste for their behavior in life, Harvey saw little satisfaction in the breakdown that many in the waiting room were now going through. One of the older men could be seen in one of the brightly lit corners masturbating, his pants barely hanging off his ass, his underwear exposed. Harvey started to feel for the group. He never gave his life over to anything with pure blind belief, only moments of drugs, women and his writing. An old Catholic women knelt, fondling a rosary and begging God, in the last hope of validating her belief, to give her a sign. When none came she simply collapsed on the floor.

Across the walk, Muslim women were ripping off their veils as frantic husbands begged them to stop at once. One of the husbands became aggressive and slapped his wife, a young woman no older than twenty years of age, across the face. She looked at him stunned at first but then pulled out a knife from under her dress and pressed it against the his throat. She screamed something in Arabic which Harvey could not understand, but the point was clear and the husband sat down with his arm folded with a huff.

He walked on, passing old men in hospital gowns with newspapers under their arms. Walking on the other side of the corridor was a group of teenagers with bullet holes in their clothing. He moved past each gift shop and gate, some empty, others full and still others strewn with sparse passengers waiting to get onto their bus. Sounds of crying infants echoed throughout the terminal along with the occasional bark of a dog. Children, ran from room to room, often knocking over the elderly and fragile showing no remorse. As one kid with long blonde hair sped past, Harvey stuck out his foot, tripping the boy. The teen looked up at Harvey his fists balled with anger before running off to find his friends. Tripping the boy was an empty gesture, an attempt to hold onto a bit of himself which seemed to be slipping away in this afterlife. There was no humor or sorrow to be found in an event that would soon be forgotten.

Former squeegee men smiled with toothless mouths like wise men of a loser's corner, knowing that the days of begging were now over. The terminal was the great equalizer of men and women and didn't matter if one was buried above ground or Potter's Field. The meaning behind the social tiers had collapsed. For some it was a grim reminder of how fragile power is. It's a lesson that should have been learned in 1929 when millionaires, bankers and those on Wall Street woke one morning broke and threw themselves out of their office windows, dying like the young girls leaping to escape the fire at the Triangle Shirtwaist Factory.

The announcements were now coming every five minutes when he noticed, much to his joy and horror, his Aunt Julie from Long Island, who had died 19 years ago from breast cancer, was heading out the exit. Without thinking Harvey made a mad dash for the door which lead to the boarding area for the buses. He ran up the line until he reached his aunt, a woman to whom he had never been close. Thrilled at the sight of a familiar face he greeted her with a smile. A woman standing behind her asked her who he was.

"He is my nephew. He has no idea what he wants." With that she walked forward and onto the bus. Two rather large employees ushered Harvey back into the station. He collapsed onto one of the seats, crestfallen with the last words of his aunt still reverberating in his head, *"He has no idea what he wants."* It was true, of course.

Despite not being tired, he was surprisingly filled with an energy which he had not known since he was a kid, Harvey decided it was time to shut down, so he closed his eyes in a post morgue meditation. It was just that the images around him and the events of the day were becoming far too much to take in; his death, the gates filled with Africans with mining dust on their faces from a western operation, the children with cadmium between their finger nails and gasoline on their breath, the women with mutilated vaginas. In between announcements came the voices of Muslim women, their tongues vibrating like rattle snake tails. He took a deep breath of the scentless air.

Harvey saw himself alone on a subway car going to an undefined station. He looked across the tracks to see another train across from his own. In one of the cars he saw someone sitting alone. "Dear God." It was him, looking down on the floor. He stared for a minute, the only sound was the wheels moving along the rail. He tried to get his attention but to no avail. A figure dressed in black came in from one of the car's doors carrying a large bowie knife. Harvey screamed and tried to warn himself of the on-coming danger but the act was useless. The stranger raised the knife over his head and plunged it right into the back of Harvey's neck, blood spurting out in a rainbow of muted death. He let out a silent scream but the scene simply faded.

Harvey shot to his feet and noticed that that the seats were starting to fill up. Some Wall Street executives passed him by, one with a sneer. Harvey continued to walk on down the infinite path of waiting areas, gift shops, bars and gates for waiting buses.

In one waiting room, dock workers sat huddled laying out their plans to unionize the afterlife so that artists and the blue collar workers aren't stuck working the sewers once again. There is the fear that the wealthy will always be able to buy themselves into the best resorts where young Indian kids serve them lightly iced drinks with umbrellas. The workers had been in the station since they were beaten or shot down with Rockefeller's hired guns.

Across from them, Japanese peasants waited for their rides with charred flesh still hanging off of soft skulls. They were the nightmares of an American past, still celebrated today under the shadow of old glory.

Part 2

Harvey made his way back to the bar where he filled out his papers. To his amazement, both his beers were exactly where he left them. He sat there for a time before a young thin Latin kid with long black hair pulled back in a pony tail sat next to him. Both of them sat in silence for a while until the stranger turned to Harvey.

"Hey man, what happened to you?"

Harvey didn't answer.

The kid didn't seem to notice Harvey's apprehension in having a conversion about his or anyone else's death.

"Yeah I killed my old lady," the stranger started. "You see it wasn't my fault, man. You see, she had this guy friend that would always show up when we were having our problems."

The kid took a drink of Harvey's dark beer before he continued. "You see, we were living together for two years, two fuckin' years man, and this little bastard would show up every time we had some troubles. She claimed that she felt sorry for him because he was in a fuckin' wheel chair. So one night I'm waiting for her to come home and its getting late. No phone call, no nothing. So it was 1:00 in the morning when she strolls in the door. I asked her where she was..."

He wiped the tears that were starting to swell in his eyes. "So she says to me, 'I told you I'm going to see Kevin tonight,' which was total bullshit because she never mentioned it to me. So I ask her…" taking another sip off of Harvey's beer, "what were they doing and she said, get this, 'we were having drinks at a bar in a hotel!'"

Streams of tears started rolling down the kids face as he told the story but he continued between sobs. "I had this thought like out of that movie, when that gangster pushed the guy's mother down the stairs in her wheelchair, doing that to the lousy motherfucker. He knew the deal that they were only suppose to be friends. But what do I do, I grabbed this gun out of my dresser drawer that we had for some reason, we both hated guns, and without thinking I shot her in the forehead. Then I put the nozzle in my mouth and blew the trigger. You know women will do that to you."

Harvey listened, horrified at first, but soon became sympathetic. The kid's face was young and he had an uneven beard. He looked upon Harvey with trusting eyes as if he had found a longlost father.

"Look kid," Harvey started, "it wasn't this guy's fault. After all he didn't do anything that she didn't allow him to do."

Harvey took a drink from his light beer before continuing, "I'm sure there was a lot more in your relationship that you're not telling me. It's obvious that your relationship ended without you ever noticing it. What's so screwed up is that one person always knows the relationship is over before the other person. That's what makes break ups such a bitch."

The kid looked angry at first but seemed to understand. "By the way," said the kid, "did you see her around? She's white, with glasses and a bullet hole over her left eye."

Harvey shook his head "no" but promised to keep an eye out for her. The stranger finished the last of the beer that he stole from Harvey and then hurried out of the room.

All the names he once knew began to fall away, becoming too far off to remember, all but one, Sophia. Harvey felt a sudden longing for her as he finished the last of his drink. He ordered another round, finished both beers and then ordered another. The thoughts of their first meeting didn't run like a film but, rather, like a series of still frames. She had been living in the Montague house after short stints at rooming houses and in extra bedrooms in the homes of strangers who paid her little mind. At night she had worked as a stripper in a Hell's kitchen club. Her job forced her to dodge stalkers who bought into the come-on that marks every stripper. Some of those who had been washed out of the pipelines of obsolescence like backwash and into the bars, had allowed themselves to fall for her. They often thought her dancing looked more like a vaudeville act than a dance of seduction, all she needed were spinning plates at the end of a stick. The younger guys were indifferent but the older ones fell in love with her.

One case however, got out of hand. He approached her one night, seemingly more charming than the most. He told her that he had worked on a ship for the local coast guard. She went along with his story and hung on him that night as he bought her drinks. After that though, when she came home, she would find him waiting for her on the stoop just outside her building. When she would come home from dates or taking care of her sick father, he would be there waiting for her. For protection, she kept a can of mace on the edge of the sink in her room. After several attempts to get the police involved, only to be met with blank wall of apathy, she left her job and her room down on 14th Street where she would fall asleep listening to the noise of heavy traffic. She would find a job working as a clerk in a medical office.

As it turned out, Harvey was nearing the end of his career as a doorman. On the good nights, old Jewish women would offer him meals while he sat at the front desk. More often though, sharp dressed businessmen in $2,500 dollar suits would come in and out of the buildings high on coke. A few times he would be threatened by those in the grip of a drinking bender. Harvey had dared to ask their guests to sign in. Shortly before he left at night, the maintenance men would disappear and invariably he would have to take care of an emergency, before the other doormen arrived. At night he would return to his room, bitter and exhausted. When he grew restless, Harvey would walk over to the Hudson River, past the art studios, iconic diners where old men sat at counters with coffee cups on stained napkins and plates of corn beef sandwiches in front of them, past high end restaurants, music stores, transvestites coming out of the rawhide bar, hustlers with their backs pressed firmly against the wall and so on.

Harvey and Sophia met one day while walking over the Brooklyn Bridge. Their conversation started with a great indifference which signified a lack of wanting anything from the other. As they reached the end of the bridge, both realized that they had a certain, undefined fondness for the other. Harvey had turned to her in one of his usual bitter moods and stated he couldn't figure why anyone would fish out of the Hudson. "Factories have dumped so many chemicals in the river I can't believe they still eat those damn fish. Well at least they can find each other in the dark, the blue glow around them will probably help." She started laughing to herself.

The discussions then turned to politics and life in the City. Two weeks later they would go on their first date, which, as it turned out, was the third anniversary of 9/11. Early on she would cry after sex and constantly had to be assured that she wasn't disgusting. The first time he had spent the night at her place, she revealed to him that she had to take medication for depression. For Harvey, the landfill that was her room was the more disturbing scene.

Truth was that he spent time in St. Luke's after two failed suicide attempts while he was in the middle of an emotional breakdown upon learning that his girlfriend of six years was leaving him for a cop.

Harvey was in the middle of a fit when he tried to overdose on pills. The details of his time in the hospital started to collapse, the muddled screams of the girl down the hall, the dead eyed negro who wandered around the rec room, striking the keys on the piano and then walking out of the room. There was the kid who had threatened to kick the door of the ward down if he didn't get his medication, "I'm starting to lose it, that bitch is going to give me my meds or I'm going to kick that fuckin' door down! One of two things are going to happen, the door will break or my leg will!"

He grew afraid of the night. Every so often he could hear the echoes from the screaming of Charlie "the vacuum" as he was strapped down in his bed. The sound of an iron door would follow and then silence would return to the ward. Unfortunately for Harvey, they would keep him drugged, unable to speak or move but all-too awake. When he closed his eyes, neon fairies shot across his eye lids until morning.

Charlie got his moniker from the staff who would constantly have to pull him from the bathrooms. Wing, a small mute Asian kid, was his favorite target. Charlie, who stood around 6 feet and was built like a biker would follow him into the bathroom stalls. Charlie would use one huge hand to keep Wing on the toilet bowl as he went down on him. The small Korean would struggle but to no avail. He would take several slaps across the face as a warning to keep still. Usually a passing staff member would hear the noise and moments later, a group of workers would be dragging Charlie back to his bed. But that was a long time ago, and Harvey had been feeling well since the last time he was hauled in.

Suddenly the string of images seemed to snap like old film and faded to black. The high heel boot of madness had been lifted from his throat and clarity flooded his senses for the first time. Only an egoist at this point could claim superiority over those who he walked among in this dumping ground where everyone is a nameless asshole. For him, the horrors from behind the heavy metal doors that separated the wing from the outside world, the screams from behind the shadows, which echoed off bare floors and institutional walls were now over. Truth was that those behind those metal doors needed no pity nor Saints but simple understanding and the occasional blow job.

Over the next two years at the Montague house, he would discover strange characters who stood at the fringe. They were painters, musicians, yoga teachers, performance artists. Unlike so many others who now walk West 86th Street, their love seemed pure and for once Harvey felt at home. There was no judgment here, most of those around him, as well as Harvey himself, understood how the wealthy and *nouveau riche* looked upon them but it did not matter. This was his tribe, the children on which the city had turned its back and sold off to the landlords, many of whom felt the betrayal of the world's indifference during World War II or those that took advantage of an American dream gone wrong. Everyone in Harvey's tribe was a Jew or Indian of the 21st Century, always being forced from their homes, but willing to fight to the last hour.

When he first told Sophia about what he saw in the hospital, she felt far less insecure about taking her medication. The two would lay on her day bed, among 12 years of garbage and regret. Two years, later they would marry out on Long Island. Harvey picked his head up from the table and got up and walked out of the bar. He passed the kid with the ponytail. His girlfriend had found him at last and was screaming at octaves not meant for human ears.

The bullet hole was still visible but surprisingly enough, took away nothing from an otherwise pretty face. The kid looked at Harvey as he passed and smiled, he found a love that could overcome the inflection of death. Yes, she was punching him in the chest and screaming profanities at the top of her lungs but, hell, they would work it all out.

"Die, die nach Berlin, Ihr Bus gehen, kommen zu Flugsteig 88D"

Harvey stumbled back towards the gates until he reached a quiet waiting room which was all but empty. Only an elderly man, with a bottle of malt liquor sat in the middle of the room. Harvey fell into one of the chairs, half drunk and in no mood for conversation. In a moment of clarity, he saw his life before Sophia starting to fade from view. Harvey was no longer of time or space, a thought that made him nauseous as he started to vomit from fear. The sensation was warm but not all altogether unpleasant. He could feel his emotions splattering onto the floor. His connections to addiction suddenly started to disappear and for the first time as long as he could remember he saw clearly that his love for Sophia became more pure. But fear also dredged up his suspicion that he had spent his life wasting time.

"Fuck," he thought. "What does it mean to be alive when you're always sleepwalking, be it because of drugs, women, or the psych ward at Saint Luke's or making plans for which you prepare but never finish?"

It was this fear which made Harvey break a sardonic smile, as he wiped spit off his bottom lip with his sleeve. He realized that there was no one to punish him for a wasted life nor were there any treasures for being anything special. And there were no debts to pay to a score keeper who watches in silence as desperate lives go up in the blue flame of chance.

But the moment of clarity was broken as the old man started talking across the puddle that now separated them.

"Where are you headed?" he asked.

"Home," Harvey answered. "You?"

The stranger didn't answer at first but just sighed deeply.

"I'm waiting for my daughter," he finally answered.

"Are you expecting her soon?"

The old man shook his head. "I've been waiting for fourteen years." He then took a swig off the bottle. "She's not showing up."

"Well she has to show up at some point. Were you two close?" Harvey asked.

"I haven't spoken to her in over 20 years."

The two sat in silence for a while.

"So what happened?" Harvey asked to break the uncomfortable quiet.

"She went off with a guy who I didn't particularly like, don't-cha know. So we had a big fight and that was it—she left. I guess I became too much like my old man, don't-cha know—too much of a strict Christian."

The old man took another drink from the bottle.

"If we think that we built any favors in heaven, then we're fooling ourselves. What are we but monkeys who can read the New York Times? Some of us can even do it without moving our lips. And we consider ourselves superior somehow to those around us and yet we still have a need to be subservient to some great God. Tell me where is God? Is he hiding in the bathroom? What good is a cross around the neck here…"

Before he could finish his sentence, another announcement rang out.

Those going to Missouri your bus will be arriving at gate 5a, I repeat, your bus will be arriving at gate 5a.

"Well that's me," said the old man and got up and walked out of the waiting room past three Rabbis yelling at each other in Yiddish, and then out of Harvey's view. After a while Harvey left the room himself and walked down the long corridor, past the gift shops, gates and waiting bodies and everyone else looking to move on.

Sold Streets

Did you know that
the city only exists in the eye of the projector.
It's film is becoming far too thin
and ready to crumble
and the streets are sold.
The projectionist is on the way out.
He found an eviction notice on his door this morning.

The beauty queen of glamour magazine
1983
now lives under the scaffolding of 91st street
beneath the thumb of AIDS.
But the tides of good fortune could not carry her away
far enough
from the streets
and sidewalks
and rooming houses
which are exposed
when those pools of fame
run dry.
Now she wears the face of disease
which
came on
like beauty's final curse
as vicious as a female preying mantis on Broadway.
Here
ruin presses against the skin
leaving its mark
like a fingerprint on still glass.

Under the watch of millionaires row
of West 86 Street
the Dexter House does not sit
quietly.
Its' children
know only night

waking at 4 in the afternoon
to walk as silent shadows who pass by
on Riverside Drive
to sustain the winds off the Hudson river
which beats against their sides
as an invisible friend.
Most live with
winter in their hearts
as the disgrace
of landlords running
unchecked grows
as a decaying threat
while others
perform at Penny Arcade's.
All have given up
looking for something
to keep clean
in cleansing fire.
Those who live behind
these section doors
are often forgotten by time
while replacing sleep
with the voices down the hall
where bathroom doors sit open
waiting for the next causality.

Wanda is frantic again
looking for the soul
that she lost in a downtown
Brooklyn
bar
where it still lies
stained
by the boots
of those squatters
she once laid.

In the side of the city
empty storefronts
sprout
like cattails over a polluted heart.
with For Rent signs pressed
against their windows.

Housing court has become
a collection agency for the landlords
judges are nothing more than overpaid clerks.
There is no defense for SRO tenants
working class
regular apartment tenants
squatters
or section 8 tenants.

Witnesses to the crimes
of iron jawed landlords
pass by
with deep seated contempt
or fish eyed indifference
then vanish from memory
as they reach the end of
the set.

Untitled

Everything you're looking for
is sitting in the room right next to you.
There is nothing behind closed
and silent doors
where the air is
still
thick
and the sun shines
through the window like a stripper
who dances at 12pm
on a Monday afternoon with no witnesses
looking on in the dark.

Matthew Abuelo

Otto and the Bug

Otto Berger lay awake staring at his ceiling, watching the shadows which were cast by street lamps and cars and passing pedestrians. This was another sleepless night in a long string of sleepless nights. In his room, the pipes started banging as they filled with air and steam that acted as a precursor to the hiss from the radiators. It was a comfort to him like a friend or a long lost lover who decided to stop by unannounced. He didn't have many visitors over at his place, being so small and cluttered. He spent most of his time there alone. He did bring the occasional woman over but never with the expectations of seeing them again. It takes a special kind of metabolism to withstand this kind of isolation, to break down the long hours of being alone and shit it out into moments of productivity as a writer. It is an art when even the telephone becomes a mute device.

Outside his door, he could hear his neighbor coming home while speaking too loudly on her cell phone for such early hours of the morning. Moments later, the door to the common bathroom slammed shut, the rusted metal sound of the sliding lock and the water from the shower head prevented any real chance for silence. Next door, he could hear the old man Jose who was in the middle of another coughing fit which woke up his dog. The little bastard started barking, "Shut up!" the voice from next door yelled with a thick Spanish accent. But the barking only grew louder. Four stories below his window, rats could be heard fighting among mounds of trash.

Two stories up, Beth a local musician was in the middle of another breakdown. She would piss in a beer bottle and throw it out the window where it would shatter among the garbage bags and the tiny wars between rotten and roach, hotel worker and drunken sickness, all under the street light theater. If she was to be found out again, in her screaming battle just to keep the last of her clarity; it would mean another weekend in Saint Luke's psychic ward. But it was the screaming born of her madness which could be heard from every open window and waken ear. *"Which one of you mother fuckers pissed on the toilet seat!?!"* which created a chill in the air.

The iron doors to the wards sit open for her as she dances through like an A list actress walking into her favorite restaurant. "You don't have to show me where to go! I know the routine. I'll be here long after you're gone."

The noises from outside his room were not the cause of his insomnia nor was it the anxiety of being at the same job too long while feeling himself self falling away. It was a buzzing sound that came from under the floor boards. It wasn't loud but the pitch was just at the point where ignoring it was impossible with its long droning sound like a mating call of an insect. It had become the most important sound of the night and morning. The first time he heard it, Otto thought it was a piece of electronic equipment which had fallen under the piles of newspapers, empty movie cases and clothes strewn across his floor. When he didn't find anything there, he lifted his mattress with one hand, and with the other, rummaged through the piles of garbage which had long been forgotten about. With disgust, Otto let the mattress drop. He made every attempt to ignore the buzzing which seemed to move across the floor. As he lay there, it felt as if the sound was reverberating inside his skull. This started three days earlier. In a fruitless attempt, Berger turned on a lamp by his bed then got up and lifted his mattress in more desperate attempt to find the sound. With one hand, he moved the clothing and papers underneath the bed from one side to the other. The heavy smell of dust shot up in his face. It was a gray smell, like that of an old abandoned factory, or a construction site. It was a smell with weight which could be felt making its way down to the lungs.

Otto's eyes started to water as he coughed profusely gasping for air. He dropped the mattress then grabbed a shirt from the corner of his bedpost and tied it around his mouth and nose. After the coughing fit was finally over he looked under his bed once more but found nothing. Black spots shot across his eyes from a lack of sleep. He had grown used to the numb feeling that came with being awake for too long, and the headaches from the bright morning light. He even had come to terms with the long hours of being alone with only his voice to keep him company, but the drone was getting to be too much to bear.

He lay back down with his head at the foot of the bed and took the shirt from around mouth. The sound suddenly became muffled as it continued to move under the floor boards. Otto's eyes started to close for the first time in several nights. He felt his body becoming relaxed. Sleep started to take him. But then the noise came on louder than ever. He turned over and saw a large five inch cockroach, sitting on an empty bottle in the middle of the room. At first, he wasn't sure if the insect was real or something born from the darkest region of a bad dream. He had never seen a creature like it in his waking life.

Otto looked for his shoes in hopes of stepping on the vermin. When he couldn't find them, he slowly reached for a board that he had leaning on one of the walls near the bed. He moved slowly as not to excite the invader. As he pulled it onto the bed the roach jumped off the bottle and scurried to one of the only exposed spots on the room's floor. With one motion, Otto threw the board onto the bug and in one motion, jumped off the bed and landed feet first onto the board. He stood there, applying pressure in an effort to kill the thing. Suddenly the board started vibrating violently. He almost lost his balance but managed to catch himself.

The vibration stopped and there was no noise other than the garbage trucks announcing the morning. The first light of the day shone through his window. He lifted the board and the roach ran under a dresser on the far side of the room.

"You little bastard!" Otto grumbled.

Taking care not to make noise himself, he moved the piece of furniture to the side. There he saw a large hole where the floor met the cracked wall. Berger grabbed a can of raid which sat within reach on a cart. He was about to spray inside the opening but stopped.

"What if a colony of these little monsters come racing out of here like rats on a fix?" he thought.

His situation could get quickly get out of control. With that, he walked to his closet and from one of his jackets, Otto grabbed a lighter. He then moved back over to the hole. His plan was now set. He sprayed a quick burst down the hole and then waited for something to come out.

The roach poked his head out. No not yet, Otto thought. Not until the red of his thorax is visible.

The insect started to slowly crawl out of his sanctuary, clearly dazed by the bug spray. Berger lifted the lighter and the can and shot out one long blue flame which caught the creature at point blank range. It turned around and raced back into its hole and under the floor boards.

The vibrations from the baked bug's back and wings were now coming through in broken waves. Otto dropped to his knees, exhausted and now too weak to keep the fight going for much longer. The noise of night was replaced by the sounds of day. Juan could be heard next door moving around clumsily while getting ready to take his dog for a walk. Voices could be heard from the air shaft. Some belonged to the buildings workers while others were those of tenants on their way out to work. Berger collapsed on to his back, his head lay on a pile of clothing and magazines. His eyes rolled back into their sockets as his body became slack. The buzzing sound soon faded into the back ground.

Images of his childhood started to appear like fish in still and stagnant waters. His old man had joined the military shortly before he was born which meant no roots were able to form any where. Every two to four years he and his family would be in a new town, new city, or new country. One Christmas they would be in Hamburg, Germany, the next they would be in Olympia Washington. The experience sent his older brother over the edge as he dove into drugs and started hanging out at some of the local fringe clubs. Otto started to do the same when he reached his teenage years. He swore that he would never follow in the old man's footsteps.

Here he was though, in a single room chasing down a roach. The scenes started to change. Soon Berger was standing at the bottom of a garbage chute. From above, strange high pitched sound could be heard like an old PA system with the microphone too close to the speakers. He looked up and saw a large roach pushing burning newspapers down the chute.

Otto rolled over and was awakened by a deep green smell, like the moldy odor from a poorly aged cheese. He didn't open his eye right away but he felt something crawling on his hand. The all too familiar sound rang out louder then ever, even closer than before. It sounded like an electric saw on metal. He was now wide awake.

Otto looked down at his hand, "Goddam bug!" he screamed and grabbed the heaviest thing which he could reach, a hard cover encyclopedia of insects which an ex-girl friend had given him, and slammed it down on the intruder and his hand. The pain of tiny jaws biting into his skin shot up Otto's arm. In a fit of pain, he grabbed the bug, squeezing it with all he had. He swore that he heard a high pitched scream from the bug but threw it across the room, where it struck the wall, leaving a green mark before bouncing onto the bed.

To Otto's surprise the bug had survived the impact, and crawled slowly behind the bed. A dull pain started over Otto's right eye. It was the headache of one who hasn't slept for three days. He slowly stood up then made his way to his bed. As he got up, the pain shot to the back of his skull which forced his eyes to close as if he had lost all control over them. When he made it back to his bed, half blind, he collapsed.

He suddenly found himself alone with his thoughts. A depression set over him. The wounded pest was his first guest in days and the only one willing to stay around, wanting no commitment in return or phone call in the morning. He dared to allow himself to weep softly for his fallen nemesis. The roach gave him what no one else ever had, the greatest fight he had ever known. For the first time in recent memory Otto Berger had to pay attention to something over which he had no control. As he started to drift off, the buzzing sound rang out from under the bed, then grew softer before there was complete and perfect silence. He could tell from the one last attempt by the roach to be heard that it had crumbled in defeat and was now gone. Soon he stopped weeping then slipped into the deep waters of REM sleep.

Moments later, his alarm went off, it was 8:30 am. It was now time to join another battle in a long string of lost battles.

The Silent Screen

All the porn houses are closed down now.
Projectors stare blindly
into the vacant theater
like an empty gun
with no more images
left in the chamber
as the film finally snapped
from the pressure of those streets
wiped clean of all memories
of those who died just to keep it
all together.
Those faces have vanished
into the silent screen.

They are
the marks that sit at
lunch counters
with coffee stained napkins
always waiting
for the game of chance.
All shows canceled.
All young women who loved
old and lonely men are gone now
with retirement plans
and full benefits
They no longer know
the neon signs
that read
private booths in back.
There are no award shows
for the naked theater
only a pass to the Tombs.

2

All the ideas have become too ordinary
and accepted.
Artists now live above the streets
no longer willing to dance
through the metal doors of the psych wards
where angelic ideas are born
in
sanitized halls.
"You don't have to show me where to go
I know the routine. I'll be here after you're gone."
The academies have castrated the word
turning all meaning into a blue mist of
barren winter on the written page.
Its all advertising now.
dead images
of beauty's
final curse.

3

The brown snow of the east continues to whitewash the crime
which the city was built on.
The Wall Street deals.
The back room deals.
The race track deals.
The under the table deals.
The off shore deals.
Turning housing court into
a collection agency
where judges do the work
of filing clerks.

4

Do you know the stories that sit on the curb
in garbage bags
from rooms with eviction notices on
SRO doors
Working class doors
Coffee house doors
tenement doors.
and the doors of ghosts
which no longer shatter under the pressure
of putting on a good performance
in a booth
on the other side of the glass.
Now they
perform
under the Hudson moon
just beyond the reach
of old men
who forever will
feed 10 dollar bills into slots
and sit on plastic chairs
waiting for the show
which never begins.

5

Only the truly wealthy can afford
to forget
what has already been buried
in Saint Luke's
on Potter's field
on Fresh Kills landfill of Staten Island.

6

New York City,
once the kingdom of misfits,
now sits like an empty store front
with For Rent signs pressed against the glass.
or the last great porn star
presenting herself to those lined up
on the other side of the camera.

A Song for the Ages

When your fortunes
are all spent
And you sit in a
Westside diner
Over a cup of coffee
Waiting for nothing
Because there is
nothing left to expect
But those dreams you
once thought
tamed now bare their teeth
and turn back on you.
Your boss tightened
the screws on you
The only thing that
waits
At the front door
are eviction notices
as you wash out onto
the street
on the aborted tide.
New York is a dead museum.

Opera of Lust

Young school girls
pass by like ghosts
of our first lay
in the back of abandoned houses
in upstate New York
just out of the reach of the street lamp's glow
and nameless.
Their thighs
are soft confessions
of silent lust
but
their trust comes at a price
to know the debt
of losing
your name
in the game of chance.
To spend the night in rooming houses
where the air carries
the weight
which turns the mind
to that of a confused animal
with the wish to be nameless
or perish by that name
which will be added to a list
used
as
the end
of
a
whip.
Here guilt
is recorded in
the record of the body
where our soft lust is not a fix
but always ends with a felony.

Discussion Guide

The News Factory is a collection of poetry and short stories that takes a look at the lives of those people and places that are quickly vanishing from New York City. The characters in this collection include, the artists of the Upper West Side SROs, the homeless former model who was once featured in *Glamour Magazine*, who is now battling AIDS. There are also several references to corrupt city building inspectors and the hell that they cause. My aim for this work is to keep alive those memories of what the city once was, the iconic home for outcasts, artists, so-called weirdoes and what Studs Terkel labeled, referring to characters dreamed up by Nelson Algren "losers still clinging to a dream." But mostly this collection of poetry and short stories are a celebration of their lives, as well as my own, having gotten to know those who I consider the real geniuses of the city.

1. What effect does the author feel that gentrification is having on the working class in New York City?

2. What does the author mean when referring to modern New York as a "dead museum?"

3. What does the author imagine will be the long-term effects on the city's artistic community with the loss of affordable housing?

4. In "The Bus Terminal" the main character, Harvey Gray finds himself in the port authority of the afterlife where most of the waiting rooms serve as statements to the chaotic choices and situations that people often find themselves, along with the perceived injustices of power. Do you think that the various examples mentioned in the story, i.e. the frantic Christians, Muslims and homeless along with union members have any connection to each other?

5. What do you think Otto's mental state says about his relationship to the bug?

6. Sex workers, strippers and their voyeuristic audiences are a recurring theme in the poems as in "Silent Screens". What do you think this imagery represents to the author?

7. In "Revolution of Trash" what does the author mean by "the Jerusalem of their hearts?"

About the Author

Matthew Abuelo is a writer, professional blogger and award winning poet best known for his observations on life in modern day New York. Born in Manhasset in 1975 to a father enlisted in the military, he and his family travelled throughout most of his childhood, living in army bases across the United States and Germany. After an early stint as a counselor for special needs children, Mr Abuelo began focusing more attention on his writing, developing his skills beyond poetry, to other genres including fiction and journalism. As an activist he helped organize the StrapHanger's campaign to fight for public transportation in Nassau County in the 1990's, has been involved in various campaigns within the peace movement after the invasion of Iraq and Afghanistan and has worked as an affordable housing advocate in New York City. Living in an SRO on the upper west side inspired him to write about his friends and neighbors, the remnants of bohemian New York, struggling to survive in an increasingly hostile and antagonistic world.

His two previous books *Organic Hotels* and *Last American Roar* are available on lulu.com. A former journalist for the online news site Examiner.com, Mr. Abuelo currently writes for the *Times Square Chronicles*, a bi-monthly publication based in Hell's Kitchen.